SICK NOTE

&

SCRAPBOOK

Andy Botterill

CW01496716

APS Books
Yorkshire

APS Books,

The Stables Field Lane, Aberford, West Yorkshire, LS25 3AE

APS Books is a subsidiary of the APS Publications imprint

www.andrewsparke.com

©2025 Andy Botterill

All rights reserved.

This is a work of fiction. Any resemblance to actual persons, living or dead, places and events, is entirely coincidental.

Published worldwide by APS Books in 2025

A catalogue record for this book is available from the British Library

SICK NOTE

Something Missing ~ 3
Priceless ~ 4
Day Trip ~ 5
Life Partners ~ 7
Angel Of Mercy ~ 8
Another Time Another Place ~ 9
Absent Friend ~ 11
Delayed Shock Syndrome ~ 12
How Fickle Love Is ~ 13
Alienation ~ 14
A Free Country ~ 15
Poison ~ 16
Mid-Life Crisis ~ 17
Ghosts ~ 19
Not Much Of A Man ~ 20
Sally's Wild Years ~ 22
The Learning Curve ~ 23
Asylum ~ 25
Silent Yearning ~ 26
When It's Over ~ 27
Sick Note ~ 28

SCRAPBOOK

Details ~ 31
Moving Parts ~ 32
Rum And Blackout ~ 34
Making The Best Of It ~ 35
Pillows And Sheets ~ 36
Beatnik ~ 37
Clowns ~ 39

A Different Person ~ 40
Play Things ~ 41
Graduate Dilemmas ~ 42
Still Birth ~ 43
Mob Rule ~ 45
Coming Out ~ 46
I Wish ~ 47
This Life Is Hard ~ 48
Virgin Manoeuvres ~ 49
Enough ~ 50
Glass ~ 51
Crossroads ~ 52

SICK NOTE

SOMETHING MISSING

He was happy once, and then she left him.
He didn't know when he was onto a good thing.
That was his perennial problem.
They had a house. He bought her a kitten
and showered her with gifts of love,
and then took them all back again.

They used to go to town on a Saturday evening.
They drank until they could hold no more,
and more often than not it was fun.
Sometimes they'd choose to stay in.
They'd buy fish and chips and eat them
on the sofa in front of the television.

Later they'd make love with the light on,
and they'd talk in hushed, affectionate tones
until night became morning.
He knew how to hold her attention.
That is until she found another man.
Suddenly she stopped giving and stopped being so open.

She said she needed something new
to open up her horizon. She said
he was no longer the person he'd once been.
It was hard to take in.

Now he is alone. He thinks of her from time to time.
He remembers the days they spent together,
but all in all he's got used to her not being there.
He's met other women, but somehow
they weren't quite the same.
He tries to make it work, but something's always missing.

PRICELESS

You'd meet if you didn't have this other bloke.
I'm sure of that, for all your protests
that is has no bearing on us.
I ask only that I'm allowed one more chance
to cast my eyes on your face, to hear your gentle voice,
to touch your cheek, and yes, to kiss.

It's not much, but it would mean a lot.
By denying me even that small request,
You make it an unattainable target.
You've elevated its worth
to something out of reach I can never afford.
Indeed it's become priceless.

DAY TRIP

It was a cold day and we decided to go to Budleigh,
to while away an afternoon by the sea,
getting some fresh air in our lungs,
and doing things a little differently.
I drove the twenty odd miles slowly.
We were in no particular hurry
and got there about three if I remember correctly.

You complained that you'd worn the wrong shoes.
The hard pebbles hurt your feet you said.
They felt rough under each tentative step you took.
I told you not to worry and not to get upset.
It was only a short distance from the car
to a bench where we could sit.

We lit cigarettes and vowed to give up
at some unspecified date in the future,
but knew in our hearts we wouldn't in fact.
We bought hot dogs and drinks from a dimly-lit kiosk
and walked hand in hand along the beach,
emptied by the sharp chill of early winter.

Later it snowed. The breeze blew small, icy flakes
into our faces and made them red.
We held each other close, afraid to let go,
as if once parted we'd be separated by the wind
for all eternity and could never be reunited.

On the way home I stopped the car.
We stared out over Woodbury Common for over an hour,

trying to estimate the distance between us and the moon,
and comprehend the meaning of that small place in time
that was us, together and forever
at that moment, and nothing more.

LIFE PARTNERS

You've stitched me up good and proper this time.
You say it's my fault that we now live apart
and perhaps you're right, but it doesn't help
or make me feel any better for all that.

You led me down a blind alley, a dead end,
a narrow track that just petered out, I think you will admit.
You said one thing and then went ahead
and did something completely different instead.

You said you needed time on your own,
to gather your thoughts, to sort out your life
and get new interests. That's a laugh.
You didn't say anything about finding someone else,
which is all you've done in fact.

Evidently your promises mean nothing.
I shouldn't have placed so much faith in them.
It's only a matter of weeks and months
since you said we were partners for life.

I didn't know life was that short.
We obviously have very different perceptions
of time and space. That's the complex answer.
The simple one is you lied through your teeth.

ANGEL OF MERCY

He did his best and offered them advice
as and when he could, even when they chose to ignore it.
He still loved them underneath,
for all their disappointing traits and unworthiness.

He tried to show them wrong from right
and keep them on the straight path.
He made it his mission in life to spread joy and happiness.
He said he'd lead them into the light,
as they wallowed blindly in darkness.

His promises were too much to believe
and they laughed openly in his face.
He didn't mind. He was unconcerned about himself.
He gave them love, for what it was worth.
They responded by cutting off his angel wings
and nailing him to a cross.

ANOTHER PLACE ANOTHER TIME

It's always the same.
I sit at home all day with nothing much to do.
The records I play only make me sadder
at the prospect of carrying on without you.

I have a comprehensive record collection.
The songs of Joe Jackson and Van Morrison
still bring tears to my eyes ten years after first hearing them,
but there's just no one close enough to dry them.

This time I've dug myself a real hole to wallow in.
I watch the thin, black vinyl spinning on my second-hand
turntable
at precisely thirty-three and a third RPM
and wish life could have the exact same precision.
It's hard being alone, but I recognise I'm not the only one.

I like to keep my options open.
I try to keep in touch with what's happening,
dropping in on other people's lives from time to time,
through magazines, the radio and television.
There's always someone home.
You just have to tune in to find them.

I get a kick out of Pete Sampras winning Wimbledon
and the US Open, as if I'd hit every ball for him.
But when it's over, I come back down.
The view from my room hasn't changed.
Morning and evening still come,
with little to break the dull monotony between them.

I thought I was a good person, so why then
did I torment you with the vicious passion that I did?
Why did I wrap myself round your every nerve,
so you couldn't breathe or release my grip?

Did you suffocate for me?
Did you bleed so that I could live?
Why did I reduce you to a physical wreck and a pale imitation
of the person you'd been when we first met?

If I knew all the answers to every question,
I wouldn't be where I am.
I'd be somewhere altogether different,
in a better place and another time.

ABSENT FRIEND

I love this place. My only sadness
is that I have no one to share it with.
For that I blame the girl who walked out
just months before I made the move
that was meant to reshape my life
and give it new direction and impetus.

I suppose I'm saying it's her fault
that my happiness has been tinged with remorse,
or am I being too harsh?
I just find it odd that my new flat
and the existence I have now built for myself
have her presence engraved in every aspect.

Her soft voice and the memory of her face
form the bricks and the mortar
that keep it together and hold it in place,
for even in her continued absence
she shapes my destiny like nothing else.

DELAYED SHOCK SYNDROME

It's called delayed shock; what you see on my face.
I suffer from it a lot. It's a type of illness,
with symptoms and pains like any other.
There's just no cure. Only time is the healer.

It's not like a cold or the flu. You don't only get it
during certain seasons of the year, say winter.
It can strike you down morning, afternoon or evening,
in hot or cold weather, and often when you least expect it to.

It happens when someone tells you something you don't
want to hear;
that you're through when you want it to last forever.
It doesn't sink in at the time. You just say fine
and carry on as normal as if nothing has happened.
You hear the words but guess you were mistaken
about their true nature and meaning.

A month later it hits you with the weight of a stone,
like you've just been told you've got cancer.
You can't move. You can't do anything.
You think it's temporary paralysis that you can't raise your
arm
and you can't pick up your coffee cup.

In fact it's delayed shock you can't get to grips with.
That's all it is. There's no secret in that diagnosis,
but it doesn't make it any better or less acute
or any less worthy of treatment.

HOW FICKLE LOVE IS

She said she'd follow him to the end of the earth,
do everything he ever asked and give him everything he ever
wanted.
He said she loved him too much and shouldn't say such
things.
They were naïve and foolish and she couldn't possibly mean
any of it.

She responded by smothering him in kisses,
to prove she spoke the truth.
She bought him expensive gifts and made outrageous
promises
about the totality of her fondness.
She said he was the only thing in her life.

Then she found out he'd once loved someone else.
It was hard to accept at first, but after she did
she quickly took back every word she'd ever said to him.
It had all been a huge mistake, she explained
by means of excuse, as she packed up her things and left.

Now she lives with someone else, whom he presumes
she also showers with empty promises.
Such is life, he sighs with a tinge of regret,
as he's left to reflect how fickle love is.

ALIENATION

If I could see myself as others do, I would be very sad.
If I saw someone in my position, I would pity them.
I would tell them there's no point in going on,
but I can't pity myself however much it makes perfect sense
to.

I see this single room I have as a palace. Don't tell me it's
not.
Don't tell me it's just part of a giant concrete block.
Don't tell me the view I look out onto when I get up
is in fact nothing more than a mirage.
It would break my heart, but then you did that without any
thought.
Why should it be any different now we're 200 miles apart?

What you sow is what you get I suppose.
The only thing in you at least I thought I'd made a good
choice.
Now you tell me I'm wrong. That's a shame.
That was all that was keeping me going.
It's a sobering lesson, and one that's hard to learn.
I suppose I was mistaken then in thinking
even your loathing was better than nothing.

A FREE COUNTRY

Mid-morning comes; these days the alarm no longer rings
to wake me from my slumber at seven sharp like it once did.
I should have been up much earlier perhaps,
but I have nothing of meaning to get up for.

Morning is not what it was when you were still here,
but I don't miss the shrill whistle of the alarm clock,
shattering the dawn still and forcing me
to get out of bed and make breakfast at all.

When I go to bed I have no need to set it,
not anymore. I have no need to time my life
and tie the day's dullness down to seconds and minutes,
as if every moment counts, when at least for me it doesn't.

I lost the job some weeks back.
That was my only real reason for going out, but now it's
gone.
It was probably a mistake to leave on a sour note,
but I have no regrets on that, even though the bills are
mounting up.

I lie in bed until late. There's no point getting up,
and I don't have the energy to shave
this scraggy beard that's grown across my face.
All right, our relationship just didn't work out.
I know the truth, but I haven't got over it.

Allow me that much. Allow me a little grief.
I know I shouldn't indulge my self-pity in this childish way,
but it's my choice. It's a free country.
If it wasn't, I wouldn't have let you leave me like you did.

POISON

You've changed. You look the same,
but your voice has altered its tone.
Where once it was soft, now it's harsh
and your words are laced with venom.

I know. I've felt them. I've endured the pain.
You're a different person to the one
I once held in such high esteem.
You've spurned my affection, tossed it aside
and thrown it back at me again.

You're no friend of mine. You can't be.
If you were you wouldn't keep hurting me
like you have done. You'd throw me a lifeline,
but you prefer to watch me drowning.

I sense I've lost this one, but I keep hanging on
for some reason I can't quite explain.
I still seek and treasure your loving.
All you give me in return is poison.

MIDLIFE CRISIS

They did it as nicely as they could in the circumstances.
They told him he'd had a good innings and done the
company proud.
He had a fine record, built up over many years of loyal service
to take with him to his next job, whatever that was.

They were apologetic he had to leave,
but said it was best for all concerned.
He'd be sorely missed, they were quick to point out,
but hoped he understood why they could no longer keep him
a place
in the current flagging economic climate.
He'd find something else. They were quite sure of that.
His kind of skills and vast experience
were something richly valued in a competitive employment
market.

They even gave him a parting gift
and a modest redundancy settlement.
They held a party in his honour at the office.
They gave him a hearty pat on the back
and wished him good luck in his future ventures.
They said it was a shame that business had got so slack.
It was nice, but somehow it wasn't quite enough.

He was confident at first. He was only 49.
He was hardly over the hill, he thought.
Surely his record would stand him in good stead for another
job.
He even had the odd interview here and there at first,

among the rejections that arrived with a dull thump
on the mat every morning when he got up,
but he never got any further than that.
Somehow his face didn't quite seem to fit.

A chill wind has blown through his life.
They had to give up the house in the end.
They said goodbye to it one rainy afternoon.
It was hard, but there was nothing else to be done.
And the car and home entertainment system were eventually returned,
when they couldn't meet the monthly repayments on them.
Finally to add to his woes his wife walked out on him.
Yes, after 25 years of good, solid marriage.
She knew how to kick him when he was down.

He started drinking. He lost weight.
He suffered headaches and dizziness.
His doctors failed to identify the cause of his vomiting.
They thought it must be stress that was doing his head in.
Now he drinks alone in a small, rented flat
on the east side of town, contemplating what he did wrong,
what the future holds, and whether he's got one.

GHOSTS

You had it done then; a 60-dollar perm,
new wardrobe and expensive shoes on your dainty feet.
Looking good doesn't come cheap these days,
but what sense does it make in the grand scheme of things?
As if changing your appearance and clothes
is enough to erase all evidence of us.

It was foolish to think that I fear.
It takes more than a simple makeover
and a clear out of your room to change the past.
You have to dig deeper, but even that is insufficient.

You can have a shower, but even that won't wash off
the essential essence I left. You can change your hair,
but I shall remember it how it was.
Getting a new job is great,
but it doesn't make you any different underneath.

Sure, you can move house if you wish.
You can get a trendy, new apartment.
You can buy yourself a dog, a rabbit, a mouse or a cat.
You can do lots of things to change your life,
but you can't blot me out altogether.
I shall be like a ghost who'll haunt you
for the next ten years at least.

NOT MUCH OF A MAN

It seems quiet in the house since he left.
You thought other women were hard to find
in this neighbourhood, but he found one all right,
sly, old dog that he was.

Funny how you didn't notice the little tell-tale signs
staring you in the face all too obviously in retrospect;
him going out late and not coming back;
the occasional excuse for a letter or phone call you hadn't
expected.

You didn't think he was the type. That was your mistake.
You thought him content with what he had –
a nice home and a loyal wife, everything on a plate,
and the easy life for him if no one else.

You always made such a special effort
to keep everything in its place,
to iron his shirts, to press his trousers just as he liked,
to do the dishes, the garden, the housework, and now this.

At least he waited until the children were grown up
before making his sharp exit. That was a small grain of
comfort,
although it didn't end the gossip. That hasn't stopped,
and you still can't face the neighbours or hide your
embarrassment.
It still hurts too much, even though some months have now
passed.

Yes, it seems quiet in the house since he left.
You didn't think he had the nerve, but he did.
He wasn't much of a man in truth.
It's just someone to talk to you miss.

SALLY'S WILD YEARS

They were mad, sad, drunk days,
when everything was more alive.
You were my first lover and together we made sweet music
in a rented apartment on the Lower East Side.

Beer ran like water. You preferred gin if I remember.
We drank until we could hold no more, falling asleep
just as others got up in the half light of dawn,
to eat greasy, cooked breakfasts and go to jobs we didn't
have.
Yes, it was simpler for us in the wild grip of youthful love.

They said it wouldn't last, but I knew better of course.
I always did, or so I thought at least.
Perhaps sex clouded my judgement, or was it just drink?
Lust is a tonic few can resist, and if it was my undoing
in the end, hell was it fun while it lasted.

THE LEARNING CURVE

I thought about her every day when she first left me.
Now not so often, in fact only occasionally, I'm sorry to say.
Funny how even true love gets diluted
without some small sign of potency to keep it topped up
and to maintain its drive and energy.

Yes, it happened, despite all my good intentions
and the promises we made and have since broken.
I wavered from my masterplan, mainly out of self-pity
and a growing sense and feeling of rejection.

I found I couldn't keep myself solely for one person;
not for someone who didn't return my phone calls,
who left my letters unanswered, who didn't share my longing.
I turned elsewhere in the end, perhaps a little too soon,
perhaps more than a little out of desperation,
a need for someone to rely on here
and not 200 miles away in London, who didn't care.

I had no desire to relieve myself
of the commitments we'd made to each other,
but alone I had no option, if you'll pardon the admission.
How I wish I was better at what I do than I am
and that I could hold her attention with my charm,
that I could capture her imagination
and absorb her totally with a wealth of imagination.
Alas I can't. I don't kid myself. I'm just not that kind of
person.

I should have done it all differently
the first time and at the first opportunity I had.
I haven't been given the chance
to learn from my error of judgement.
That is the harsh lesson I take with me into this new liaison.

ASYLUM

It's time. It's half past ten.
It's the same thing every morning.
They're letting me out for a half-hour break,
as is the routine, as is the custom,
that's been established over time,
to have a walk, to stroll around a bit,
to get some exercise while I can.

I'm allowed at least 100 yards in this direction,
maybe fifty yards in that, as far as the perimeter gate,
up to the apple tree and back, if I want,
but no further, no further than set out
in the rules that dictate the running of this place.

It's you who's done this.
It's you who's done this to me sadly.
You said you wouldn't get nasty, but you did.
You were as nasty as you could be.
They're trying to send me mad.
Is it surprising that I scream a bit,
that I can't swallow my food, that I wet my bed?

I had a wife and a kid. I had a wife, a kid and a job.
Now I have none of it, but a straitjacket and a noose to fit;
electric shock treatment, as much as I can take.
I've learnt to love the crack of the whip on my back
and the tube forced down my throat.
Yes, thanks for that, for your contribution,
and for giving me asylum when I most needed it.

SILENT YEARNING

It would never have worked. I know that.
I wanted kids. You alas did not.
I knew the day would eventually come
when it would be time for us to part,
but now it has, I'm still filled with regret.

It's the little things that I miss most,
like waking you up, bringing you breakfast,
watching you laugh as you once did,
but my yearning remains silent.

I miss the phone ringing. I miss its shrill tone,
greeting me as I get home from a hard day at the office.
You were always so precise about time.
You never forgot a date and were never
a minute early or a minute late.

I miss your voice and soft lips.
I miss your warmth in my bed,
but most of all I miss a potential wife
whom I've let slip through my fingers
not for the first time in my life.

WHEN IT'S OVER

When it's over you just carry on as before.
You pick yourself up, dust yourself down
and brush the cobwebs from your hair.
When it's over you slip into town for a beer.

Coming to terms with the end of a love affair
doesn't become any easier with the passing of the years.
In some ways it gets harder.
You worry you've messed up your last chance
to make something of a relationship
and to achieve happiness, whatever that is.

You consider yourself foolish for getting into it in the first
place.
You consider it wasn't worth all the stress and heartache it
caused.
Most of all you blame yourself for the hurt and the way it
ended.
You're not sure if it was your fault, but you guess it probably
was.

A month later you lie in bed with your new lover
and wonder if anything has changed.
She has different coloured hair.
In some ways you like it better. In other ways
you wish she was someone different altogether.

SICK NOTE

I've lost faith in my body these last six months.
It's started to let me down time and again.
Where once it was strong,
now it's weak and in pain.

It began with just little things;
the odd cold and flu-like symptoms.
Now they've increased to full-blown illness,
but I continue to defy the odds.

I remain in good heart.
I still go to work,
and I shall not give up,
for where there's life there's hope.

SCRAPBOOK

DETAILS

It's the little things you notice. It's down to the details.
That's what makes it work or makes it fall apart.
They make the difference, whether it's employment, love or
marriage.
It's the little things that make the tragic comic and the comic
tragic.

When you're up, you can laugh about it.
When you're down, it's the opposite. You just can't shake it.
You try hard, but that mood has a will of its own.
You can't contain it, despite your very best attempts
to wrest control back and be master of the direction your life
takes.

I blame the weather. When it's warm I'm all right.
When it's cold and wet I'm not. Somehow I'm different.
It's just a little thing, the weather, when you think about it,
but it's important and can determine our mood.
Yes, I blame the weather when I should perhaps
blame myself that I'm in this mess.

I can always go to the pub and get pissed.
I can go to a football match. I can do whatever I want.
I can even shake this pain from my heart.
I can even erase the memories of the one I loved.
Firstly, I just need to be sure that's what I really want.

MOVING PARTS

Sevon o'clock, the alarm rings, telling me to get up.
I do all the usual things; wash, shave, dress, eat breakfast,
all at the same time as yesterday
and the day before that, and the day before that.

The daily routine has become imprinted on my mind,
like a record that won't stop playing
or a television programme that keeps going back to the start
again,
except there's no new twist and no new storyline to keep it
going.
It remains the same each time.

At least I don't have to think too much.
It requires no special effort on my part.
I can transfer myself to autopilot and allow my body
to follow the pattern that has become established
and do the rest for me. I can continue to sleep.
My limbs move but my mind doesn't.
It needs more pressing matters to stir it.

I shut my front door and walk out onto the street.
It's only a short journey to work and all its mystery has been
lost.
The postman makes his deliveries like clockwork.
The milkman calls at each house but mine.
I see the same cars pulling out into the road
and slowly driving off into the distance.
I notice the same faces looking up as I pass them.
They stare impassively into my eyes and I stare back,

with neither love nor recognition.

I find myself reading the same signs, banners and posters
as I have a thousand times or more and wonder why I do it.
I wish I could break the routine, but I know I can't.
The programme has been set and the die cast.
I'm just one moving part. I can't break out.
It would upset the overall balance and equilibrium of things,
causing everything else to stop, grind to a halt and never
restart.

RUM AND BLACKOUT

It's going to be a real session.
We've got the booze in; everything you can imagine -
beer, cider, whisky, vodka and wine.
We'll finish the lot, no problem.
We'll knock it all back and polish it off,
until there's nothing left, not a single drop.

Me and my mates have been planning it for ages.
We'll have a bit of a competition between us,
to see who can drink the most and who's got what it really
takes.
I've promised that Barney Riggs I'll drink him under the table
and I mean it. I know I can. He can't hold anything inside
him.
He's no real man. Five pints and he's gone.
Not like me; I can drink anything.

I'm a bloody alcoholic I am.
There's no stopping me once I get going.
Just keep them coming and I'll neck them down.
Pints, glasses, shorts and shots; it's all the same.
Just you see, you lot are a bunch of lightweights compared to
me.
Until a few hours later when all the bravado has gone.
Puking over a toilet rim, it doesn't seem quite as clever then.

MAKING THE BEST OF IT

As she walks down the street she pauses to look at herself
in a shop window as she saunters past.
She looks different to how she did.
She's put on weight and resents each pound.
She remembers how she was before she became pregnant
and she wishes she could go back to that.
If only she could turn back the clock, but she can't.

She wonders how she did it. It surprised even herself.
She'd always been careful, except that once.
She'd gone over and over it in her mind, time and time again,
and that was the conclusion she'd reached from all her soul-
searching;
that the man it must have been was now somewhere else.
He was just passing through and without doubt was long
gone.

It was partly her own fault she has to admit.
No strings and no ties she'd always said
to each one of the men who'd walked in and out of her life,
but she hadn't counted on this particular situation unfolding
as it had.

She's going to give birth to a kid,
but is little more than a child herself.
She still wants to have fun and go out.
She wants to dance and get drunk.
She wants to date, but she can't.
For her it's all in the past and will remain there.
She's stuck in a one-bedroom flat by herself
and has to make the best of it for the foreseeable future.

PILLOWS AND SHEETS

They say it's a sin, but that's how I feel.
I feel angry deep down. I feel angry at you for what you've done.
Walking out on me at the first sign of a problem
was a dirty trick. I blame you that I live alone.

It's your fault that I have no one to go to the pub with.
It's your fault that I eat by myself,
that I get up and go to work in stark, empty silence,
and I hate you for it I must admit.

Oh how it's churning me up inside and taking hold.
It's enough anger and resentment to last a life.
By now I should have been married.
I know that and I blame you that I'm not
and that I'm still left here on the shelf.

But what really hurts more than anything else
is the thought that a new lover
now occupies your bed, whilst I just have
pillows and sheets to rock myself to sleep with.

BEATNIK

I hate following the crowd.
If other people like something, I don't I'm afraid.
That's just the way I live my life. It's my choice.
Where I can I keep myself to myself.

It's unimportant whether you agree with it or not.
I don't want to follow in your footsteps or anyone else's.
I want to make my own fashions and set my own trends,
whether it's lifestyle, clothes or music.
You won't find me in those High Street shops.
I don't go to popular places.

I want something a little different is what it is.
I want to stand out. I want to get noticed.
You can call me alternative.
You can call me what you like.
It won't make any great difference.
I'll never do things your way if I can possibly help it.

You can keep your safe, little job and your house.
You can keep your car, your 2.4 children and your mortgage.
I'd rather be out on the road with the wind in my hair
and a fast bike beneath my feet,
or shacked up with a hooker in some two-bit dive,
having sex day and night if I could.

I don't like commitment. I don't like working hard.
If you want a job, that's nice, but don't force me into it.
It doesn't fit the image. It doesn't go with the haircut.
It doesn't match the jacket I choose to wear.

I'm sorry if you don't like my attitude, but that's just me all over.
I don't try to conform or please anyone.
In short I'm the veritable ghost of Jack Kerouac,
come back to walk this planet one last time.

CLOWNS

It was a mistake, but I can only blame myself.
I was warned against falling for someone
who worked in the circus when it came to town,
but I did. I still did it alas. God help me,
I couldn't stop myself, for all my shame and regret.

You lived life in the fast lane. That's how we met.
I found it hard to keep up with the pace you set.
You left me short of stamina and fighting for breath.
We didn't communicate in words, you threw knives instead,
or pulled another rabbit from your hat.
You made me walk the tightrope in your footsteps
and laughed as I tripped and fell flat on my back.
You could be cruel like that.

You left me confused. You had me all tied up in knots.
You left me wondering what was an act and what wasn't.
You wanted me to tame lions to prove myself worthy of your
love.
You said I would if I was serious about engagement and
marriage.
I tried. I swallowed swords to show I spoke the truth.
I mastered the trapeze, but it wasn't enough. It was never
enough.

I thought that I loved you, but you were just a tease.
You left me wondering what other tricks you kept up your
sleeve.
I thought I could contain you,
but I found I wasn't alone in sharing your bed.
I thought I was an artist, but I was just a clown instead.

A DIFFERENT PERSON

He beats her regularly. He beats her almost every day,
but she stays with him. She has no choice she feels.
She's not exactly ugly, but she's not exactly pretty either.
She worries she wouldn't get anyone else if she left.
It's better than being alone, isn't it?
Besides, she's now carrying his baby.
If only for the kid she feels she must stay.

He beats her regularly.
Sometimes in the morning before she gets up
and sometimes at night. He beats her almost every day.
It's her fault. It must be, she tells herself.
She's doing something wrong. She only annoys him.
If only she wasn't so useless.
If only she was good at something,
he wouldn't have started drinking.
He'd be a completely different person.
She tells herself this, but who is she kidding?

PLAY THING

Your force is so strong.
You're like a magnet puling me in.
You're all consuming.
There's this physical and emotional attraction
I feel towards you that will not be broken.

Yet I'm scared to get too close, lest I be entrapped,
like a fly on a spider's web or a mouse in the paw of a cat.
I feel I'm just your play thing,
but even that's better than nothing.

I try to maintain my distance, lest I be scorched
by the strength of the heat you give out,
but still your flame burns inside me
and I can do nothing at all to stop it.
You've implanted your seed and it's taken root.
I've been branded by your mark.
The trouble is it feels so good.

Your radiant eyes are like a cool, blue lake to bathe in.
Their colour is so fresh, vibrant and refreshing.
I find them hypnotizing. I am controlled by your endless
fascination.
You only have to say the word and I will do anything.
My body yearns for us to be as one.
So just open your heart and I'll pour myself in.

GRADUATE DILEMMAS

They never tell you what it's really like.
Be a good boy, study hard, and you can do anything you
want.
I did all that; O-Levels, A-Levels, no sweat!
I even added a degree on top.
I thought I was the bee's knees, I did.
So why do I have this overwhelming feeling of
disappointment?

Working in an office from nine to five isn't all that bad.
It's just not what I expected.
I thought I'd be on TV or working as a disc jockey.
I had hopes of getting a deal with a record company.
I certainly didn't expect to be the teaboy,
but that's what it feels like.

Even now as an adult I can't answer anyone back.
I can't say what I really think.
I only speak when asked for a response.
I just nod at all the right times in all the right places.

That's why I'm getting out. I've had enough.
I'm going to take a chance. I'm going to live rough.
I'm going round the world from start to finish,
and if you don't like it, that's just tough.

STILL BIRTH

It's never mentioned. We don't speak of it.
All evidence has been erased.
The cot, the kiddies' clothes and the soft toys have all been
sold.
I've even changed the front bedroom back to how it was,
before we put all that *Winnie-the-Pooh* wallpaper up.

I've returned the baby's blankets we borrowed.
The pushchair has gone back.
I've buried myself in work. I've tried to forget.
I've tried not to blame myself,
but I can't help wondering if things would be different
if I'd got you to the hospital quicker than I did.

All talk of babies and children is banned from the house.
They are something we thought of, but can no longer have.
We maintain a dignified silence.
We avoid the subject and steer well clear of it,
but the past still conspires to come between us.

You never gave birth to anything living,
but the miscarriage has still left an emptiness
that can't be filled despite our best efforts,
as if something had lived, when in fact it didn't.

I try to comfort you with a kiss, but you just turn your head.
I sense you resent even my touch.
I didn't wish to put you through this,
but it couldn't be helped. It was no one's fault.
I wish I could make things better, but I can't.

I suggested we adopt, but you wouldn't hear of it.
It wouldn't be the same if it wasn't your own
flesh and blood you said.
I see your point, but what other choice do we have?

I fear you've given up and lost all hope.
You say you're now incomplete and it can't be put right.
I accept that. You make a fair point.
It's bad enough that we can't have a kid,
but what's worse is they had to cut bits out of you like they
did.

MOB RULE

I'm a clever one I am. You need to be in this game.
You have to keep your wits about you
all the time or you'll end up like them,
in some backstreet with a hole in the head.
It's like that here. You need to be harder than the next man,
to stay ahead of the game and be leader of the pack.
You need to carry a bigger piece and not be afraid to use it.
I've wasted a few in my time, with no remorse and no
recrimination.
It's just business. It's nothing personal, man.

I run my team, the gang, with a rod of iron.
They know the rules, every one.
They know what will happen if they let me down.
I have a reputation. I'm known on the scene.
Drugs is what I deal in, and the occasional paid killing.
It's easy to whack them. They'll never be missed in this part
of town.
Believe me, if you have the nerve, you can do anything.
I'm a god in this life, a king, but if I make it to the next one,
I'll surely fry in hell for all I've done.

COMING OUT

I can't tell them. I just can't.
Bloody parents think I'm as straight as an arrow, but I'm not.
It will bloody kill them, old fashioned as they are,
that their only son is not the same.
I can't tell them that I don't like women. I like men.

I've tried dropping hints, but it doesn't work.
They don't take any notice.
Surely they suspect something's up.
I'm twenty now and still never had a girlfriend.
It will come, they say, if you keep trying.
Don't you worry. You'll get one in time.
I don't bloody want one. I want a man!

I'll have to tell them eventually, but when?
This can't go on indefinitely. It can't go on forever.
Sooner or later they'll have to know the truth,
however much it might hurt to do so.
It's dad I worry about. He's very much a man's man.
In his day he was a right stud by all accounts.
He knew how to put it about. So do I, I think,
but in a different direction if you get my meaning.

I like men. I don't like women.
It's easy to say when they're out of the room.
It's when they're here that I have a problem,
but hold on. Who really has a problem here?
It isn't me. It's they who are in the wrong.

I WISH

I loved her, but she was no good.
I treated her badly, but mainly she brought it on herself.
I tried to make it work. I did everything I could.
It was just hard. It didn't work out.
I just wasn't her type. I know it.
I wish I hadn't said those things, but I did.
I wish I hadn't knocked her about in the heat of the moment.
I wish she'd stayed faithful, but she didn't.
I wish I hadn't found her in bed with another bloke.
I wish all of this was different.
I wish she was still around.
I wish she hadn't walked out.

THIS LIFE IS HARD

I wake up every morning the same,
lying drunken in some gutter or other.
I can tell if it's summer, autumn or winter
by the temperature of the air on my hands,
neck and face, and the stiffness of my hair.
It was cold last month.
Thank God it's now a little warmer.

I shuffle into a sitting position,
before rising unsteadily to my feet.
I seem to wobble as if I've been hit.
The street spins for a moment beneath.
Slowly my eyes come into focus and I'm awake.
This life is hard. It really is.

How long it's been since you threw me out
I no longer know in truth. I used to keep a note.
I'd jot it down on an old card piece I carried.
Now all that has been lost,
victim to the dirt and filth I'm surrounded with.

I've been beaten up more than once,
but mostly I'm left alone by myself.
I'm too dirty to touch. I should carry a sign saying as much.
It's a protection of sorts on the streets.

I take pleasure in the simple things.
That's all I have left to appreciate.
I shake myself off and get some
much needed oxygen in my lungs.
I'm thankful just for getting through another night
and I go in search of breakfast.

VIRGIN MANOEUVRES

It was his first time, fumbling in the dark for a condom.
He wasn't even sure how to put it on.
She was bound to notice his inexperience,
his general air of panic and incompetence.

He cursed himself. If only he'd asked
someone with more knowledge and awareness first,
but it was so hard to admit, wasn't it,
that he hadn't actually done it before.

He said he had of course.
He'd bragged to his mates.
They thought he was a right stud, but he wasn't.
He was a complete novice at all of this.

Hell, he couldn't even open the packet.
That was difficult enough,
let alone put the bloody thing on his sagging erection.
Should he quit? Should he keep persevering?

Is there something wrong? she asked.
You have done this before, haven't you?
Of course I have, he replied.
I've just had a bit too much to drink.
You know how it is.

Almost eighteen and still a virgin.
He was nearly a man
and this was his first time with a woman.
If it was always going to be like this,
he wouldn't bother again.

ENOUGH

She looks in the mirror and wonders
if she's putting on weight.
She disgusts even herself.
If she hates the sight of her own flesh,
how could anyone else love it? How indeed!

She lights a cigarette and reflects
what a repellent habit that is in itself.
She wishes she could make friends and go out,
but she has no one at all to go out with.

Her man spends all his time with his mates.
He stays out late. He has a pint and a laugh.
He knows all about the good life.
She has none of it. She's shackled to the flat.
She has housework and washing up.
Then it strikes her how ridiculous it all is.
At last enough is enough!

She puts on her hat and coat
and slips quietly out into the night, heading for a club,
wondering if she'll ever go back
or if she's saying goodbye for good.

GLASS

You are glass. You shatter to the touch.
The merest word said and I fear you'll break.
A remark or a comment out of place
and all too easily you will smash.

My dear, why didn't they make you differently?
Steel would have been better, even wood, but alas you are
glass.
Your silver shards tear my skin when we touch,
I barely notice at the time, only afterwards.
You're still in me, even when you're 1,000 miles away.
I feel the proof, the hurt and the pain.

You are too precious and too vulnerable for a mere mortal
man.
I can't stand the way you break down
at the slightest hint of an argument.
I want a woman, not a piece of porcelain or a vase,
something for the mantelpiece alone, but you are glass.

Yes, glass can break, but it's also sharp,
like your harsh words and sharp tongue.
You're not the only victim.
I've come to appreciate I'm also one.

CROSSROADS

He gets home at six every night and has tea by himself.
There was a time not so very far back
when he would have been off out,
but he feels a little old for that.

Part of him still likes to go to a club. Part of him doesn't.
Part of him doesn't want to grow up.
Part of him wants to remain a kid,
as he feels he is inside, but at thirty it's hard.

He's still waiting to meet Miss Right.
He's had relationships, but somehow
they always break up and never work out.
He has a good job, but it doesn't satisfy his heart.

He wants to do something with his life,
but he's not quite sure what it is.
He has interests but they don't usually last.
He finds it difficult to commit. That's the crux of it,
but he must learn before it's too late and his life is wasted.

VERSE FROM APS PUBLICATIONS
(www.andrewsparke.com)

A Black Country Chap's Life Of Rhyme (Johnny 'Mogs' Morris)
A Poem From David And Other Departures (Gill Pakes)
Artists 4 Syria (Various)
Backing Into The Limelight (Pete Crump)
Bohemian Raspberries (Mark Skirving)
Broken English (Andrew Sparke)
Cobwebs In The Hedgerow (Wanda Pierpoint)
Drinkers Thinkers Outright Stinkers (Mark Skirving)
Dub Truth (Kokumo Noxid)
Edging Out Of The Shadows (Pete Crump)
Fluid Edges (David Hamilton)
Fractured Time (Andrew Sparke)
From Bearwood And Beyond (Keith Bracey)
Goddess Woman Butterfly Human (SC Lourie)
Gutter Verse & The Baboon Concerto (Andrew Sparke)
I've Landed (Empress P)
Inside Looking Out (Milton Godfrey)
Irrational Thoughts Random Rhymes (HR Beasley)
Just Pieces Of A Man (Kokumo Noxid)
Love & Levity (Andrew Sparke)
Lyrics From Life And Imagination (John Wright)
Moth Tales (Various -edited Phil Thomson)
Phantom Verses (Angela Patmore)
Pipe Dream (Kokumo Noxid)
Poem From David And Other Departures (Gill Pakes)
Poems For The Old 'Uns (Johnny 'Mogs' Morris)
Poems Of Protest Power & Politics (John Wright)
Reading Rites Writing Wrongs (Ian Meacheam)
Refracted Light (Andrew Sparke)

Riding The Top Deck (John Wright)
Shining Light Dark Matters (Ian Meacheam)
Sick Note & Scrapbook (Andy Botterill)
Silent Melodies (Andrew Sparke)
Silent Songs Of Owen Parsnip (Angela Patmore)
Still But Still Moving (Phil Thomson)
Stone People Glass Houses (Ian Meacheam)
Tea Among Kiwis (Andrew Sparke)
Tea and Symphony (Andrew Sparke)
Tequila & Me (Andrew Sparke)
The Boys Of Winter (Angela Patmore)
The Gathering (Malachi Smith)
The Highwayman, Pink Carnations and The Re-Allocated Coal Scuttle (Revie)
The Mother Lode (Andrew Sparke)
Vital Nonsense (Andrew Sparke)
Walking The Edge (Various)
We May Win We May Lose (Jim Ryan)
Wicked Virtue (Andrew Sparke)
Wild Verse (Andrew Sparke)
Word Bombs (Eddie Morton)

Printed in Great Britain
by Amazon